A BALANCED LIFE

A
BALANCED
LIFE

Prayers to help to get life into perspective

SAINT ANDREW PRESS
Edinburgh

First published in 2009 by
SAINT ANDREW PRESS
121 George Street
Edinburgh EH2 4YN

ISBN 978 0 7152 0929 5

British Library Cataloguing in Publication Data
A catalogue record for this book is available from the British Library

Typeset by Waverley Typesetters, Fakenham
Printed and bound in Great Britian by Bell & Bain Ltd, Glasgow

Contents

How to use this book

The prayers in this collection address the worries and insecurities of daily life. The first few prayers are concerned with the day-to-day demands on our time and energy, and all the worries and responsibilities that go with them. Later, the prayers reflect on our insecurities: those things in life that either chip away at our sense of well-being or that cause deeper anxiety and worry. The last few prayers in the collection reflect on aspects of renewal, allowing us to embrace life fully refreshed.

But this is only a loose arrangement. In truth, many of the themes overlap. So you can start at the beginning and work your way to the end, or you can look through the prayers to find a particular topic you would like to address at a particular time, or you can simply pick a prayer at random and reflect on its theme. The chosen path is entirely up to you.

Some of the prayers have Scripture Readings, which are there for further reflection or to allow prayer groups to discuss the themes in relation to both the scriptures and the contemporary world.

There are some prayer activities, too. These are designed to stimulate your many senses in a prayerful way. They are perhaps best used when you are alone, when you have some time away from the routine of daily life. It may be useful to create a 'prayer corner': some personal place where you can have as much peace and quiet for reflection as you possibly can. The prayer activities hope to prompt a personal response;

but prayer groups also may find that they are appropriate. You are, of course, encouraged to be creative with them, to adapt them to your own circumstances. The point is to engage with prayer, not to let it be a dull ritual.

As the prayers in this book concentrate on contemporary life, we hope you will return to them again and again and find new resonance within.

My Lifestyle

I came that they might have life, and have it abundantly.

~ John 10:10 ~

Prayer for Ourselves

I enjoy a full and active life, Lord.
Those with whom I work
>   seem satisfied with my efforts,
>   and have even been heard to say 'Well done'.
My friends have laughed in my company,
>   and been there for me when I have needed them.
My family are always at the end of the phone
>   and we have shared life's celebrations,
>   as well as life's endings, over the years.
My health, all in all,
>   has enabled me to run and play,
>   and provided the stamina to endure.
My pocket has always contained enough spare change
>   to help another in a crisis.
I have experienced
>   the passion and excitement of love,
>   – as well as love's struggle.
Both in giving and receiving

life has engaged me in its mystery,
and I am grateful, Lord.

Prayer for Others

Fill with your love, O God,
the hearts of those whose lives seem empty
of relationships that matter and jobs which satisfy.
Fill with your compassion, O God,
those who keep their fingers gripped so tightly on their
    money and belongings,
that they have forgotten how to share.
Fill with your humility, O God, those too proud to
    recognise
how their standard of living is obtained at the cost of
    another's freedom.
Fill us all with such gratitude, O God, that all may witness
    to the gift of life
with a life of thanksgiving and hope.

Lifestyle

Grant this to me, your servant: Let me live so that I may keep your word.

~ Psalm 119:17 ~

Prayer for Reflection

God of all life,
in you is novelty and everlastingness, lavishness and
    simplicity.

In me, aware of the needs of humanity
        and of the limitations of the earth,
there is confusion over what to buy,
                what to preserve,
                what to destroy,
                and how to be a good steward
                of your resources.

Because good works alone do not lead to salvation,
make me open to the prompting of your Holy Spirit.
Then may I live wisely and well.

Prayer on Today's Theme

Save us, Lord,
    from the temptation to buy what we do not need;
    from confusing what we need with what we want;
    from wasting what we do not own,
    from owning what we will never use;
    from idealising the past as a golden age;
    from bequeathing our children a sorry inheritance.

Strengthen the arm and the will
    of all who, for the good of the world you made and
       love,
    challenge our greed
    and inform us about appropriate living.
    May their words gain a good hearing
    so that the world may have a good future.

'I am the Bread of Life'

~ John 6:48 ~

Prayer for Reflection

It takes me so long, Lord,
to plan the meals and balance the diet;
and buy the groceries and cook the food.
And mealtimes are not always a joy,
especially if I feel the need of company,
or cannot enjoy the food for keeping the peace at the
    dinner table.
I need more to sustain me
than what my money buys and human hands prepare.
I need to identify a deeper hunger,
and to give you time to nourish my soul.

Prayer on Today's Theme

Help us, eternal God,
provider of all nourishment,
not to be greedy.
Prevent us from craving tomorrow's bread before today's is
    eaten;

and keep us from demanding more faith before we savour
    and cherish
what you have already given us.

Be gentle
when you touch bread.
Let it not lie
uncared for, unwanted.

So often
bread is taken for granted.

There is such beauty in bread:
beauty of sun and soil,
beauty of patient toil.
Wind and sun have caressed it;
Christ often blessed it.

Be gentle
when you touch bread.

~ Anon ~

Time for God

Jesus sat down, and when his disciples had gathered round him,
he began to address them.

~ Matthew 5:1 ~

Prayer for Reflection

I sit down, Lord,
    to watch television,
    to write a letter,
    to mend clothes,
    to rest my feet,
    to listen to music,
    to read the paper,
    to shut my eyes and forget.

You sit down, Lord
    to wait for me
    to be ready for you.

Help me, among the other things
    for which I sit,
    to remember you
    waiting for me.

Prayer on Today's Theme

I think of those who will chase the clock today,
    as if there were no tomorrow;
    and those who will watch the clock today
    as if the best were lost in yesterday.

And I think of children keen to speak
whose parents have no time to listen;
and troubled people with a story to tell
which nobody wants to hear;
and those who see time as the enemy
of their ambition,
their ability,
their complexion.

Teach us, God of eternity,
    to be kind to time,
    so that time can be kind to us.

Mary and Martha

Martha, Martha, you are worried and distracted by many things ...

~ Luke 10:41 ~

You know me, Lord, so well.
I have seen the depressing sinkful of dishes, and heard the
    laughter from the sitting room
Where the TV is; and I have wondered how I got landed
    with all this to do. Again ...
And sometimes, I've said so. Vociferously.

And I have done the dishes in a quiet house, and my mind
    has fled
To some happy or sad thought, but something real,
    something urgent
That the rhythmic swish of the dishcloth in my hand has
    set free.
And I have started, as the water from the still-running tap
Spills out of the bowl, or jumped when, in my hand,
The cup runs over.

You know me, Lord, so well.
Sometimes I am Martha, with my worthy agenda and my
    sense of being taken for granted;

My hectoring sense of all that needs done, that no one is
    doing, that drives me to ginger up and chivvy along.
The humdrum has to be got through first.
Then comes the good stuff ...
And sometimes it is given to me to be Mary.
To be grasped by a moment when eternity strikes down
    into time,
And time must yield.

Then the humdrum is charged with meaning, and not just
    the meaning of its own flat demands.
For you, Christ, are here. Now.
Help me to grasp your presence. Now.
To 'Be still, and know that I am God ...' Now.
Maybe the dishes can wait ...

Prayer Activity

Sit quietly, and look at your surroundings. Just stop completely.
Marvel at the fact that it's all there. Accept it as it is. Then, in
a way that seems appropriate to you – greet the presence of
Christ in this reality.

'I am among you
as one who Serves'

Prayer for Reflection

Lord Jesus,
all my intuition tells me that I, like Peter, don't want *you* to
    wash *my* feet;
I would rather wash *yours*.

Like Martha, I would feel happier doing something for *you*;
than think of you doing something for *me*.

But how can I know how to serve
    unless I have been served?
How can I know how to love
    unless I have been shown love?
How can I share the Gospel
    unless I have let you tell me what it is all about?

Prayer on Today's Theme

A blessing today on the servants.

A blessing on those who cook and clean, and clear up, and
    change babies, and wash clothes, and make tea, and sing
    whiles.
A blessing on those who tend ungrateful relatives, and
    listen to bores,
and re-mend what has been torn again, and repeat the
    wisdom
which one day their children will remember and cherish.

A blessing today on all your domestic servants, Lord, who
    go down on their knees in the company of Jesus.

> Bless to me the thing
>   on which is set my mind,
> bless to me the thing
>   on which is set my love,
> bless to me the thing
>   on which is set my hope;
> O thou King of kings,
>   bless thou to me mine eye.
>
> ~ *Gaelic Traditional* ~

Women around Jesus

*Many women were also there, looking on from a distance; they had
followed Jesus from Galilee and had provided for him.*

~ Matthew 27:55 ~

Lord Jesus, when you walked the earth you didn't just call
    men;
you called women too and encouraged them to follow and
    learn from you.

Let us ponder for a moment on these women:
women who followed and provided for you.
They were fortunate, given an unusual opportunity to leave
    their homes and follow their Messiah, to walk and talk
    with you.

You made them the centre of attention, Jew or Gentile,
you healed them, had compassion for them, discussed
    weighty matters with them.
When you rose, it was to women that you first appeared.
    Surely there can be no greater affirmation.

Still today women have continued to follow you, sometimes
quietly in the background, sometimes not so quietly.

Women today play many roles,
no longer just homemakers, wives and mothers, sisters and
daughters.
We pray for women who still have to fight hard to be
allowed to step out of their homes and into all walks of
life to make their voices heard.

Readings

Luke 8:1–3	*Some women accompany Jesus*
Luke 7:36–50	*Jesus forgives a sinful woman*
Luke 24:1–12	*The resurrection of Jesus*
Matthew 9:18–26	*Life and healing*
Mark 7:24–30	*A Syrophoenician woman's faith*
John 2:1–11	*The wedding at Cana*

Prayer Activity

Think of the women who have been with you on your
journey: mother, sister, friend, colleague. Take a moment to
think of what makes these women special for you, then thank
God for them and ask his blessing on them.

Mary

She had a sister named Mary, who sat at the Lord's feet and listened to what he was saying.

~ Luke 10:39 ~

Lord, we live in a different world
from the one that you knew.
No longer do families meet
and spend long hours together
talking and sharing.

The hustle and bustle of daily life,
new technologies and communications
mean that for many children living in today's world
a conversation is only as long as a text message or e-mail.

We have lost the art of talking and listening to long stories
   or debates.
We want everything in bytes, short and sweet –
preferably lasting less than sixty seconds.

O that we could spend an hour in your presence,
talking and sharing with you –
our worries

for this day,
for our families
and for the wider world.

Prayer Activity

Is there something you want to ask Jesus? Close your eyes
and try to imagine yourself at Jesus' feet. As you look up
at him is he looking down at you? He says 'do you have a
question for me?' Tell him your question and sit quietly and
listen for his answer.

Joseph (husband of Mary)

*'Joseph, son of David, do not be afraid to take Mary as your wife,
for the child conceived in her is from the Holy Spirit.'*

~ Matthew 1:20 ~

Lord, Joseph is portrayed as marginal to the gospel, with
   only scattered references.
However, within this limitation, we do know that he was of
   royal descent,
a son of David, born in David's city – Bethlehem – a
   carpenter to trade.

What sort of person was Joseph?
A conscientious Jew that kept ordinances and feasts?
We know he was good and kind;
learning the truth behind Mary's pregnancy,
he took her with him to Bethlehem, away from the slanders
   of neighbours.

Joseph must have taken Jesus to his heart, and was
   identified as his 'father'.
After the visit to the Temple when Jesus was twelve, we
   hear little more of Joseph.
Did Joseph feel marginalised and insignificant?

Or did genuine piety reconcile him to your divine will,
with a sense of wonderland peace?
Just like Mary!
Was he much older than Mary?
Did he die at 111 years of age,
when Jesus was only 18 years as tradition holds?
Whatever the truth, help us to learn from Joseph's
     life.   AMEN.

Prayer Activity

Think of times when you have felt undervalued, at work, in
the family or in the church. Picture Jesus coming to you with
reassurance of your worth as a human being, a child of God,
one of his own loved ones.

Humdrum Relationships –
Mary and Elizabeth

In those days Mary set out and went with haste to a Judean town in the hill country, where she entered the house of Zechariah and greeted Elizabeth.

~ Luke 1:39–40 ~

Perhaps, Father, when first we set out on our journey of
    faith,
We thought we were saying 'Yes!' to something
That would make life different. Exciting. Constantly
    alive ...
And perhaps – God forgive us – *exempt*
From what ordinary life so often is.

Was ever a 'Yes!' greater than Mary's,
When she answered the angel, 'Let it be to me according
    to your word ...'?
And with her 'Yes!' she embraced a mother's life. The whole
    deal.
Pride, perplexity, vulnerability, anxiety, pain – yes, all
    that;
And so much that is just humdrum.
No exemption from the sheer messiness of incarnation,
And all that that big word might mean, for God's *mum*.

Where we cling to our illusions, Father, she dispelled hers.
Where we romanticise, Lord, she demythologized.
She went to talk to Elizabeth about being a mother. The
    reality . . .

Help us, like Mary, to find the reality of Christ,
Where life is what life *usually* is:
>   Doing what needs to be done, meeting needs that
>   aren't ours;
>   Little things, not exciting, not even very elevating,
>   But scary in their sheer volume; more, we fear, than
>   we can cope with.

We thank you for a commitment to us so total, an
    incarnation so complete
That 'Immanuel', 'God-among-us', meant this for Mary;
Hours, days, weeks, years, of humdrum motherhood.
Where, Mary might well have wondered, would God be, in
    all of this?
Then, unborn John danced his recognition in Elizabeth's
    womb.
Then, she knew.

Prayer Activity

Faced with something shatteringly new – in her case,
motherhood – Mary went straight to someone who would
know and understand this new reality. Who shares your
reality with you? Who, just now, is asking you to share their
reality with them?

Joseph and his Brothers

But when his brothers saw that their father loved him more than all his brothers, they hated him, and could not speak peaceably to him.

~ Genesis 37:4 ~

Creator of Love,
you know how we need to be loved.
You know that we need to feel special, nurtured and
    encouraged,
welcomed and one of the family.
So you gave us each other: to belong together, to connect
    with each other,
to be in relationships – understood and loved.

But God, you also know how complicated love gets.
How hard it is to be open and vulnerable
– love might not be mutual.
How tiring it is to keep on loving
– love might not be returned.
How painful it is to share love
– love might be lost.

And, God, you know the thin line between love and
    hate.

Like Joseph and his brothers, we live in families
that mix love and hate and indifference.
We often can't bring ourselves to speak peaceably to those
    closest to us.
Sometimes we say nothing – and our actions speak for
    themselves.

Forgive us, God. Teach us how to be together.
Show us a way through, with the bigger perspective
that Jesus had as people loved and hated him.
Reassure us that, if we follow Christ, one day we will know
    reconciliation, deep peace and unconditional love.

Waiting

Prayer for Reflection

Eternal God,
so much in life
encourages my impatience,
    my desire for quick results,
    my requirement of an instant cure.

To be still,
to move from my agenda to your timetable
is not easy … unless I have the company of others.

Help me, therefore, to wait for the right moment
       or the right word
       or the right person;
    to wait with longing
    or, as a sign of love,
    to wait on you
    as on my dearest friend;

and to do so
in company with Hannah, David, Mary and Paul
who learned to wait on the Lord.

Prayer on Today's Theme

Today I pray for those who are the slaves of deadlines,
quotas,
short tempers
and other people's demands.
I remember those who have no time for themselves,
no time to relax
and who grow discontent when they have time on their
    hands.

Give them a love of quietness, Lord,
in case their passion for busyness
may lead them to disregard their friends,
dislike themselves
and forget you
whom we encounter in stillness.

Patience

Prayer for Ourselves

I've done it again, Lord!
Opened my mouth and thought afterwards,
acted on impulse without thinking things through,
thought the worst without knowing the facts.
At times I seem to live on such a short fuse.
Yet still you are patient with me, showing me where I have
   gone wrong,
pointing out the better way.
Teach me how to be long-suffering, and help me to grow
   in grace
so that my anger may arise out of love for others, not in
   defence of myself.

Prayer for Others

Grant us patience, Lord,
with those who are slow,
whose bones ache as we rush past.

Help us to pause with those for whom the world moves too
   fast.
May we remain faithful to those who cared for us when
   they come to need our care,
as we remember Jesus
      who had time and patience
      with a pestering Zacchaeus,
      with a persistent Bartimaeus,
      with a trauchled Martha in the kitchen,
      with a perplexed Mary in the garden.

Listening

You have ears, so hear what the Spirit says to the churches!

~ Revelation 3:6 ~

Prayer for Reflection

She said, 'I told you so!' – but I was paying no heed.
How often I listen, Lord, but don't hear.
Sometimes I'm deaf, Lord,
because I don't want to hear what others are saying.
I treat you the same way, Lord;
when you speak, I listen but don't hear.
I don't want to hear what you are saying.

But, Lord, how I enjoy telling you what I want,
what I want you to do now, for me, for others,
the problems I want solved right now,
the worries I want taken off my back.

I realise I always expect you to use your ears.
But I have ears too:
help me to use them to hear what you are saying
to the churches and to me.

Prayer on Today's Theme

Lord, you are never too busy to hear us.
Help us
    to have time to listen to our children
    with their endless prattle;
    to have time for our old folk
    with their repetitive reminiscences;
    to have time for our demanding friends
    with their boring tales;
    to have time for disabled companions
    whose speech is slow or indistinct.

Help us to make time to hear them all,
and in hearing them to listen to you.

Work

The word of the Lord holds true, and all his work endures.

~ Psalm 33:4 ~

Prayer for Reflection

With the eye of an artist,
the perspective of an architect,
>   the skill of a weaver,
>   the timing of a gardener,
>   the faith of a sower,
>   the strength of a smith,
you, Lord,
created this world in all its firmness and fragility.

Granite and gossamer,
tree trunk and butterfly's wing,
ocean and snowflake
all exhibit your design,
all are part of your intention.

O Lord my God,
how marvellous are your works in all the earth!

Prayer on Today's Theme

Protect, good Lord,
our industries from obsession with profit
        and from practices which dehumanise workers.
Provide us
with managements and unions
which measure success in job fulfilment
        rather than in points scored.
Prevent us
from overtime which undermines family life
and from unmerited redundancy.

And may the jobless be judged
according to the worth of their lives
        rather than their lack of employment.
If, in the future, there will not be
full-time work for all,
let all have some share in the dignity of labour.

Resting

Come to me ... I will give you rest.

~ St Matthew 11:28 ~

Prayer for Reflection

Sometimes I haven't time to rest.
I have my work, the garden, the children;
my friends, my neighbours, and my pets.
Perhaps
    when I am older,
    or not too busy,
I might just rest then.

Resting is such a good thing.
Even you, God, rested on the seventh day,
    busy though you were with all your concerns.
And one of your commandments tells me to rest.

Help me not to feel guilty when I rest,
but to be grateful that there is a season for everything,
a time to rest and a time to work.

Prayer on Today's Theme

We pray for those who must rest, and find it irksome:
    those who are ill and who find life wearying;
    those who have lost their job and who cannot find
       new work;
    those who have retired and who find time heavy on
       their hands;
    those who have completed their training or studies,
    yet can find no opening for their new-found skills.

We pray for those who never rest, who are always on the
   go:
    parents with young children,
    those with elderly parents;
    people whose work is so demanding
    that their feet never seem to touch the ground;
    people who think they are indispensable
    and who never let themselves off the hook.

May those who rest and those who rush
find their perfect rest in you,
their strength and their sustainer.

Sleep

I will both lie down and sleep in peace; for you alone, O Lord, make me lie down in safety.

~ Psalm 4:8 ~

O Lord God, who neither slumbers nor sleeps,
we thank you for sleep –
    for a good night's rest,
    for a blessed forty winks,
    for sweet dreams.

O God, we thank you for Jesus
    who knew weariness and tiredness,
    who could sleep in the storm –
    for his heart was stayed on you,
    who can raise us from the sleep of death.

Forgive us for
    taking sleep for granted,
    not giving time to sleep,
    sleeping when we should be awake,
    and for any sleep of faith.

Be with those who cannot sleep:
    because of illness and pain,
    because of worry and anxiety,
    because of a bad conscience.
Grant them healing, balm,
and the serenity that is there in Christ for all.   AMEN.

Readings

Genesis 28:10–17	*Jacob's dream at Bethel*
Judges 16:18–22	*Samson's sleep*
Mark 4:35–41	*Jesus asleep in the storm*
Mark 14:32–42	*The disciples sleep in Gethsemane*
1 Thessalonians 4:13–18	*Concerning those who are asleep*
1 Thessalonians 5:1–11	*Whether we wake or sleep*

Prayer Activity

Sit in a comfortable chair – perhaps before a good fire and after a pleasant drink. With no pressing engagements, no phone liable to ring – relax, and with Christ's balm, enjoy, enjoy ...

Betrayal and Trust

Cast your burden on the Lord, and he will sustain you.

~ Psalm 55:22 ~

Lord, I need a sanctuary to fly to,
where I may be still.
My life is too often a battleground:
angry voices, harshness, brutal and unforgiving.
Each day, too, often brings another bruising encounter
in the home or in the work place.
Words like weapons cut and tear and I am left scarred and
   sore.
Find me a safe place, Lord,
where I may speak with you,
a place where my trust may grow again,
even out of the brokenness of betrayal and pain;
a place where I may find shelter for a while,
then return strong again to face the world;
a place where I may call to you in my hurt,
and find myself soothed and comforted and healed.
A trusting place.

I pray for all today who need such places:
the harassed mother, the exhausted father, the frightened
    child, the bullied teenager,
the lonely, the frail, the sick, the troubled.
May each one find that oasis of calm, that safe haven of
    hope,
that trusting place where you will come
and bless them with your gentle love.   AMEN.

Readings

Psalm 55; Isaiah 35; Zephaniah 3:14–20; Matthew 14:22–7;
Luke 19:1–10

Silence

Prayer Activity

People do let us down. Sometimes it is intentional, sometimes
it is without realising. It is a fact of life we have to come to
terms with. How do you rely on God in such circumstances?
How can you keep yourself from bitterness and from wanting
to pay the other person back? Can you hand your bitterness
over to God as the psalm does? Remember a betrayal which
is current for you or a memory that still bothers you, however
dimly. Ask God to help you, and show you new ways to deal
with the feeling of being betrayed.

Garden – Loving

I have entered my garden, my sweetheart, my bride.
I am gathering my spices and myrrh;
I am eating my honey and honeycomb.

~ Song of Songs 5:1 ~

Tell me,
who would take an eternity
choosing the million flavours of peach
and not notice it pass?
Only you, my Creator.
Who would consider the patience it takes
to harmonise the subtleties of a flower's perfume
time well spent?
Only you, my Creator.
Who would celebrate that it took not a moment sooner
to compose the sound of bird song?
Only you, my Creator.

Creator,
may I find time to celebrate in your garden of wonder,
to slow down this moment of heaven
that sweeps me off my feet in love for you
from some holy recognition
too deep for words.

And if a burden is too great,
or a pain too fresh,
may that same garden wait for me
to bloom once more
into the life you shape for me,
that I might see in the waiting
the place of resurrection
calling me.

Prayer Activity

Imagine the life of a single flower and its life cycle, watching it grow day by day and then die and give up its life. Reflect on the cross and what Jesus did for us all, giving his own life. The dead flower now waits for its seed to grow a new shoot, a new plant to burst through the ground: imagine Jesus in the tomb about to do the same.

Improvements

A better hope is introduced, through which we draw near to God.

~ Hebrews 7:19 ~

Prayer for Reflection

It wasn't clear to everyone at the time that Jesus was a
   better way.
They needed a lot of persuading
to leave the old system of sacrifice and ritual,
and adopt the new way of faith.

I don't like change either.
It frightens me,
it makes me feel uncomfortable, uncertain and unsure.

Sometimes, though, I do like to learn new things
    and am grateful for what they bring;
new friends too,
after the initial worry about whether they will like me,
whether they might turn out to be boring,
or whether they are really what they seem.

Simon did not keep you to himself, Lord,
but said to Andrew, 'Come and see'.
Help me today
to bring something new to someone's life,
even introduce them to you.

Prayer on Today's Theme

Be with those who feel that new things are a threat:
the young person starting a new job
when everything is strange,
the older person at work
who cannot grasp new technologies and methods,
writers, preachers, journalists and leaders of opinion
who have fixed ideas.

Encourage those who have alternatives to offer,
newspaper columnists who challenge the popular view,
the new member of a group or company who introduces
    fresh ideas,
those who fearlessly proclaim the Gospel.

Give to us all the courage of Abraham,
who, at a word from God,
left the safety of all he knew,
and went on a journey.

Interruptions

Hope deferred makes the heart sick.
~ Proverbs 13:12 ~

Prayer for Reflection

Why is it that just when everything is going well
something happens
which not only causes a delay
but makes me wish I had never started?

Why is it that when our hopes and visions
        receive a setback
it doesn't just dim them for a little
– we could cope with that –
but often makes them vanish altogether?

Yet, Lord, you are the continuous line
who runs through all our experiences,
waiting out our bad moments
        till we recognise the encircling arms,
patient as we gradually jettison
        our treasured ambitions
        and embrace the Kingdom's goal.

Prayer on Today's Theme

To those whose scars and wounds
are invisible to the naked eye,
your touch, Lord.

Upon those whose hurt is deep,
who carry secrets they can hardly name,
your strength, Lord.

Among those who wander
without direction or purpose,
your company, Lord.

My Fears

The Lord watches over all who love him.

~ Psalm 145:20 ~

Prayer for Ourselves

Lord, my greatest fear is not
when the world will end,
    nor how,
(though perhaps it should be).

The fears which haunt me are more mundane – even
    laughable.
I am afraid of the dark, at times,
and of spiders and snakes.
And there are some things that really scare me:
I am afraid of growing old alone;
afraid that the phone won't ring tonight,
or that it will ring,
and I won't like what I hear.
I am afraid of losing my friends.
I am afraid to make commitments.
I am afraid, as are so many,
that life will pass me by

and I will be left
thinking only what might have been.
Help me today to take the risk and put all my trust in you.

Prayer for Others

God,
you are both father and mother to us all,
watch over those who are afraid.
To those who fear the night
and the thoughts darkness brings;
to those who fear a new day
with all its anxieties;
speak your words, Lord, 'Do not be afraid'.
To those who fear that they cannot cope, who consider
    themselves failures,
those so distressed they consider suicide;
speak your words, Lord, 'Do not be afraid'.
To those who fear for one they love, who is ill, or dying, or
    left alone;
to those afraid to face up to the truth about themselves or a
    relationship;
speak your words, Lord, 'Do not be afraid'.

In God's Memory

They think in their heart, 'God has forgotten, he has hidden his face, he will never see it.'

~ Psalm 10:11 ~

O Lord my God,
Remember me, remember me.
I am being torn apart;
people talk about me behind my back;
I know I am far from perfect, but their words hurt.
Remember me, remember me.
I am not being given a fair hearing;
the people that I trusted have turned against me.
Nobody understands.
Remember me, remember me.
My family know me too well;
they say nothing but look accusingly;
I feel so alone.
Remember me, remember me.
And where are you, Lord,
when my words turn to ashes in my mouth,
when my mind is in disarray and my thoughts are
     jumbled?
Remember me, remember me.

O Lord my God,
when I cannot speak or think for myself,
when the world seems against me and even you yourself
    appear to be far off,
hidden –
stand beside me,
tower over me,
wrap yourself around me,
to keep me safe from fears, real and imagined.
Today and every day,
O Lord my God,
Remember me, remember me.   AMEN.

Prayer Activity

God is always present for us. This is both our theological belief and the witness of Christians throughout the ages, so when God appears to hide, we question what is going on. One way of looking at this experience of God hiding is that it allows questions to come to the surface within us and helps us to face things which are difficult. Hold the truth of God's presence in one hand, hold the experience of God hiding in your other hand, and see if you can allow a dialogue to emerge like the one in the psalm. If it helps you, write down your dialogue, create your version of this psalm. Then ask God for discernment. Which questions are you being asked to continue wrestling with? Which are you being asked to let go of and simply leave in God's hands? Finish by asking for whatever you need to take you further in understanding and love.

Affirmation – the Touch that Healed

'Daughter, your faith has healed you …'
~ Luke 8:48 ~

The moment she touched your garment, Lord,
she knew healing, change;
you affirmed her in precious relationship.

How splendid, a double blessing:
for the body and the fearful vulnerable soul.
But her need and input mattered
to enable your work to be done.

I'm grateful that you accept me in just the same way,
your beloved child, with my acorn of faith.
Thank you for those who encourage and affirm in my
    everyday places,
who let me know I'm accepted.

There are many who have been crushed by life experience
who believe they are of no value to anyone.
I pray for your grace
to cherish them through the love of Christ,
heart to heart.   AMEN.

Readings

Psalm 139:13–18; Jeremiah 31:1–3; Luke 8:40–56; John 17:7–10; Hebrews 13:5–6

Silence

Prayer Activity

Jesus said 'Talitha cum' to Jairus's daughter. 'Talitha' means 'little girl', or 'one who has not fully realised their potential'. 'Cum' means 'get up' or 'come forth'. Imagine cradling in your arms a part of yourself which you sense God is calling forth into fuller potential. Open your arms and release yourself into his love and care.

God, the Source of Confidence

'Come', my heart says, 'seek his face!'
Your face, Lord, do I seek.

~ Psalm 27:8 ~

The Lord is my light and my salvation;
whom shall I fear?
The Lord is the stronghold of my life;
of whom shall I be afraid?

Lord,
I like these words of confidence,
and the note of trust that runs through the whole psalm.

Joyful trust! Confidence! The absence of fear!

If my father and mother forsake me,
the Lord will take me up.

God help me to live a spirituality of dignity and quiet
    strength,
mature in reaction to the things that test me daily.

You are my stronghold,
I don't need to be afraid.

You heal my wounds
and help me to be brave and strong
time and time again.   AMEN.

Prayer Activity

Where are you safe with God? In church, at home, out walking, listening to music, lighting a candle, in your own heart? Imagine being there. Allow the feeling of safety to surround you and then let it permeate your body, your bones, your muscles, heartbeat, your breath. Embrace and enjoy the sensations of safety. You have cells forming in your body every moment; bathe them in love.

Strength

Be strong and stout-hearted, all you whose hope is in the Lord.

~ Psalm 31:24 ~

Prayer for Reflection

I think of friends, staunch and true,
upon whose strength I have depended,
on whose shoulders I have wept,
who have listened into the wee small hours;
always there when I have felt broken-hearted,
building me up,
so that, burning with a new hope,
I have been made strong again.

Help me, Lord,
to recognise when someone needs my help.
Show me where in my life and experience
I can find the resources to rebuild another person's life,
and what life experiences of mine
    would stand in the way of my helping.
Help me to bring these to you
    and find forgiveness
so that I do not keep inflicting them on others
    and causing them to stumble.

Prayer on Today's Theme

I give thanks for people in all walks of life,
who pass on their strength
both to those who know them well
and to those who have never met them,
people whose work and whose generosity has affected the
    lives of many.
I pray for those who lack strength of character,
because of the way they had to grow up,
because of damaging experiences,
or because that's the way they are.

Encourage them, Lord,
        as you encouraged Zacchaeus:
show them that all have a place, and all are loved.

Myself

*I heard the sound of you in the garden, and I was afraid because
I was naked; and I hid myself.*

~ Genesis 3:10 ~

Prayer for Ourselves

How often do I find myself
hiding the real me
behind my own stubborn pride at home,
behind a display of competence at work,
behind a facade of respectability in church?

Lord,
why am I so afraid of being vulnerable,
or making a mistake,
ashamed to show that I am not perfect?
Grant me the humility to admit that I am created in your
    image,
        fearfully and wonderfully made,
that within me is sown the seed of your compassion,
        your spirit,
        your truth.

Teach me to love myself,
as you love me,
and then I can come out of hiding.

Prayer for Others

Creator God,
I pray for those who cannot love themselves.
Open the way of hope
to those who live in fearful and abusive circumstances.
Open the door of forgiveness,
to those who are ashamed of their past.
Turn your face
towards those who cannot raise their heads,
who have been stripped of dignity and power
through imprisonment, disability, abuse, prejudice;
those who have nothing to hide,
because they feel they have nothing left.

Lord Jesus Christ, who hung naked on the cross,
clothe them all in your mercy and love
and be their salvation.

Being Real

I wonder, Lord, how many people know me?
How many people know me, the real me?
I am so good at acting – expert wearer of masks, talented
   adopter of roles:
the smile that hides my anger,
the laughter that camouflages my pain, the confident voice
   that veils my fear.
Only you know me as I am.
Nothing at all is hidden from you: the tangle of hopes and
   fears,
the tension of good and evil, the struggle of darkness and
   light.
You know me through and through,
you know what I have been,
you know what I am,
you know all that I can become.
Lord, help me to be real today,
to lay aside my masks,
to give up my acting routine,

to grow towards the authentic 'me',
to fullness of humanity in Jesus.   AMEN.

Readings

Exodus 33:7–11; Psalm 139; Jeremiah 1:4–10; Hosea 6:1–3;
John 17:1–5; Romans 8:18–27

Silence

Prayer Activity

As we come to God we let down the masks we normally need
to deal with aspects of everyday living. Ask God to help you
to get to know yourself better, your depths. Can you let God
into those memories and corners where you are ashamed
or confused or in a rage? Can you voice that bit of venom
as at the end of Psalm 139? For us, like the writer, it often
takes some time before we can unmask the more distasteful
bits of ourselves. These are often initially cast outwards,
blaming other people. Can you let God examine who you
are, without trying to sort yourself out? With God's help, offer
yourself God's compassion. Not being able to receive God's
unconditional love can result in self-condemnation, which
perpetuates rather than heals, which becomes repetitive, even
addictive, rather than breaking through into new possibility
and new birth.

Accepting Failure

Some people ruin themselves by their own stupid actions, and then blame it on the Lord.

~ Proverbs 19:3 ~

Prayer for Reflection

Whose fault was it, Lord,
when I lost my temper and lashed out with my tongue,
and saw tears start in frightened eyes?

Whose fault is it if half the world is hungry,
or so many are homeless, and so many are jobless?

Whose fault is it if the Church is caricatured as irrelevant?

To whom can I point my finger?

Or should I bite my finger and hold my tongue
and share the blame I want to avoid?

Prayer on Today's Theme

Come to us in the morning,
come to us in the evening,
dirty and with holes in your hands.
Startle our polite meetings with your earnest insights;
upset our vague generalities with your concrete concern;
embarrass our keenness to apportion blame
by your willingness to take it all the way to hell
so that we can see the path to heaven.

Holy God, loving Father, of the word everlasting,
grant me to have of thee this living prayer:
lighten my understanding, kindle my will,
begin my doing, incite my love,
strengthen my weakness, enfold my desire,
cleanse my heart, make holy my soul,
keep safe my mind and surround my body.
As I utter my prayer from my mouth,
in my own heart may I feel thy presence.

~ *Gaelic Traditional* ~

Zaccheus and Jesus

When Jesus came to the place, he looked up and said to him,
'Zacchaeus, hurry and come down; for I must stay at your house
today.'

~ Luke 19:5 ~

When we feel we are unimportant and not noticed
You see in us the potential and possibility we fear to live
    up to.
You surprise us with an unexpected,
'I choose you.'

When our wealthy lives are lived out at the expense of the
    poor
You encourage us to be uncomfortable with our
    extravagance.
 You challenge us with an unexpected,
'I choose you.'

When we worry that our bodies may be too fat or too small
You see that which is deep within us and beyond the
    external.
You affirm us with an unexpected,
'I choose you.'

When the lives we lead or decisions we take make us
    unpopular
You demand we seek justice and act with mercy.
You change us with an unexpected,
'I choose you.'

So come amongst
the lonely, the small, the wealthy, the unloved, the
    unpopular.

Come
and be the guest of a sinner that by choosing us,
meeting us, being amongst us,
we may live out our lives
Challenging and changing
Challenged and changed.

Prayer Activity

Invite someone new round to your house or take them out
for a coffee. Enjoy the conversation and time spent getting
to know each other.

Calm

The storm sank to a murmur and the waves of the sea were stilled.

~ Psalm 107:29 ~

Prayer for Reflection

Moments of bright joy,
precious gems of peace and tranquillity,
these are threaded through my life
like pearls on a necklace.

Thank you for those blessed times, Lord;
they are your precious gift.
In treasuring them,
may I not overlook your gifts for today.

If things go wrong today, Lord,
help me to trust you,
to keep a calm sough,
and not to give way to panic.

Prayer on Today's Theme

For all who
    in their happiness and success,
    have patted themselves on the back
    and have forgotten you,
your pardon, Lord.
For all who
    in their anxiety, fear, and worry
    have screamed at you in anger,
your forbearance and peace, Lord.
For all who
cannot enjoy the good time
for worrying about the bad,
your wisdom, Lord.

Let us never forget that you are our friend,
sorrowing with us when we are sad,
rejoicing with us when we are glad.

Security

Prayer for Ourselves

I'm such a worrier, Lord.
Sometimes my worries are real enough,
weighing inside me like boulders.
I worry about having enough money.
I worry about my health.
I worry about people not liking me.
Other times I worry needlessly.
Sometimes I expend so much energy
just being anxious!

Yet even when my worst fears come true,
help me to remember that you are always there
and will hold my hand tightly.

Prayer for Others

I pray for those who have good cause to worry.

When landmarks have been removed,
and life does not make sense any more,
Lord, bring a sign that all is well.
When familiar faces no longer surround
and all seems strange and threatening,
Lord, call such people by name.
When some have lost confidence in themselves,
Lord, be their Rock.
When powerful waters threaten to engulf,
Lord, be a foothold and a haven.

Poor in Spirit

Blessed are the poor in spirit, the kingdom of Heaven is theirs.

~ Matthew 5:3 ~

Prayer for Reflection

I know what I know,
but not what I do not know.
So, when a wiser person,
    a different opinion,
    an alternative view,
confronts me,
I can be defensive at best
and arrogant at worst.

I am afraid, Lord,
    of the insecurity of not knowing,
    not being in charge,
    having to admit my poverty.

How can such a condition be blessed?
How can I understand
    unless I risk living happily
    with my limitations?

Prayer on Today's Theme

The day will surely come
    when those bent with care will walk tall,
    and the dehumanised will dance for joy,
    and the weary will smile warmly,
    and the stigmatised will take the centre stage,
    and those wrongly accused will be liberated,
    and those who suffer in silence will laugh loudly.

Until then, Lord, bring my life into contact
with those who know their need,
that I may receive the benefit of that company
to which you have given your blessing.

Celebration

Amazing God, there is no-one, nothing like you.
How blessed we are to know of you
and to be able to have a relationship with you.
Everything around us seems to speak and sing and show us
    your loveliness.
As part of your creation we want to join in the song of
    praise,
yet all our best instruments and sweetest voices
blended in harmony couldn't express the feeling of our
    hearts,
the joy of our souls at knowing you!
But let us try, God,
let us breathe your name and shout our excitement
and make sure we are heard.
God, we cannot contain you,
we cannot help our praise.   AMEN.

Readings

Psalm 150; Isaiah 43:1–8; John 2:1–13; John 20:1–20; Ephesians 5:1–3

Prayer Activity

Join the dance in your imagination. Have a ball! Let your imagination run riot. Dance with animals, trees, musical instruments and anyone you want to be there. Is there a pattern to the dance? What sort of place do you find yourself in? What colours are strongest? What does the music sound like? Give yourself the freedom to 'be there' and enjoy taking part and/or watching what is happening. At the end, reflect with God how this has changed, or not, your mood, your feelings, your thinking. Find a word, picture or gesture to mark the end of the dance for the moment.

The Lord's Prayer

Blessing

With a spring in your step,
and a hope in your heart,
express joy in this day
and embrace the gifts you have been given,
through Jesus Christ our Lord.   AMEN.

Healing

He said to her, 'Daughter, your faith has made you well: go in peace'.

~ Luke 8:48 ~

Lord, teach me how to experience your healing Love.
 Flow in me and through me and around me
  in a way that feeds me,
   strengthens me,
   reassures me,
  transforms me, lets me grow.
Allow your healing Love to flow through me to others
 in quiet ripples of gentle love,
  in waves whose force
  I do not know or understand.

Enable me to trust that a phone call made at
  an appropriate moment,
 a chance meeting in the street,
  a word spoken in the passing,
   can be a miracle.

Let me listen to your Word
knowing that some Bible stories
will change my life,
bring healing in me –
healing which also means wholeness, an
integration in me:
heart speaking to mind,
body teaching me intuitive skills,
a readiness to allow your creative Spirit to mould me
anew.

Readings

1 Samuel 16:14–23	*Music bringing healing*
Mark 2:1–12	*From paralysis to walking*
Luke 8:40–56	*Your faith has cured you*
Luke 13:10–17	*You are rid of your trouble*
2 Corinthians 5:11–17	*You are a new creation*

Health

When they call, I shall answer; I shall be with them in time of trouble.

~ Psalm 91:15 ~

Prayer for Reflection

It is when I am ill, that I call to you Lord,
to heal my body.
When I am well, I call on you less
to guard my health.

Forgive me
if I have taken for granted
your concern for my well-being.
Forgive me
if I have imagined
that Christians should never get ill.
Forgive me
if I have not cared for my body
as though it were the temple of the Lord;
and whatever the state of my mind or body,
let my spirit rejoice in your salvation.

Prayer on Today's Theme

On those who suffer
and wonder when there will be an end to pain
  … have mercy, Lord.
On those who wait for an operation
or fear to discover the results of recent tests
  … have mercy, Lord.
On those who have no peace of mind,
who seem to walk in ever narrowing circles
  … have mercy, Lord.
On those who are avoided
because of the nature of their illness
  … have mercy, Lord.

Guide the hands and the intelligence
  of those who heal;
prosper the work and research
  of those who seek new or better cures;
preserve the patience and skill
  of those who nurse and care;
and inform the minds
  of those who manage the nation's health.

Watch now, dear Lord,
with those who watch or weep tonight,
and give your angels charge over those who sleep.
Tend your sick ones, O Lord Christ,
rest your weary ones,
soothe your suffering ones,
pity your afflicted ones,
shield your joyous ones,
all for your love's sake.

~ *St Augustine* ~

Jacob's Well

Where do you get that living water?
~ John 4:11b ~

Lord of the living water,
images tumbling through history,
water that connects me with people of every age and nation
    and continent,

and with you,
Fountain of Life, well of depth, water that is still and
    moving,
moving and still.

Move me and still me, still me and move me,
that I may be part of the flow of your love, ever old and
    ever new.

Sparkling, recharging, refreshing, cleansing,
deepening, bringing clarity,
take me deeper into your living water.
Take me to the springs where your love wells up . . .

Prayer Activity

As you breathe in, imagine a spring of water welling up within you, up and out the crown of your head, and as you breathe out, imagine this fountain of water cascading around your body. If you open your mouth as you breathe out, it can help to give the felt sense of water rushing around you.

Choose to do this for five or six breaths or for a few minutes.

Deborah

*'I will surely go with you; nevertheless, the road on which you
are going will not lead to your glory, for the Lord will sell Sisera
into the hand of a woman.'*

~ Judges 4:9 ~

Loving God,
you create us to achieve our full potential,
you long for us to be our true selves and so worship you
rightly,
you want us to feel fulfilled, complete, whole.
Help us to admit that we have not been all that we could
be.
Let us see how we have conformed, made do, sacrificed the
wrong things.
Show us how to get out of the habits we have formed and
lazily stuck to.
God, release us, free us,
even when society puts obstacles in our way.
God release us, free us,
even when our parents and peers seem to want us to
behave this way and that.
God release us, free us, even from ourselves,
from all we try to be and don't need to be.

Encourage us to dream, to scheme and pave the way.
From now on, help us see ourselves as you see us,
help us live the lives that you give us.   AMEN.

Readings

Judges 4:4–10; Judges 5:1–31; Luke 7:36–50

Prayer Activity

Take a few steps, physically or in your mind. With a sense of
your potential, realise who you are to God and be encouraged
to live today with that knowledge.

Sand

Therefore from one person, and this one as good as dead, descendants were born 'as many as the stars of heaven and as the innumerable grains of sand by the seashore'.

~ Hebrews 11:12 ~

Wilderness – a place of wonder, of expansion, of terror, of
   desolation;
Wilderness – a state that allows great potential to be born
   within us, yet often through utterly rigorous testing
That we truly question whether we will get through it;
Wilderness – a condition that calls out deep prayer from
   within us.

Wilderness – a place of un-ending-ness;
No clear end in sight;
Goals missing or never materialising;
Monotony of every day;
Slow, plodding, getting nowhere.
How many of our days are like this?

Sand, sand and more sand;
Barrenness, no purpose, no meaning.

And God said 'I will indeed bless you, and I will make your
    offspring as numerous as the stars of heaven and as the
    sand that is on the seashore.'
God speaks poetry and inspiration into the very fabric of
    the wilderness.
God places a treasure, which invites a change of
    perspective that transforms unending desert into infinite
    potential – from lack and distress to hope and promise,
Even when I cannot see the promise fulfilled – yet.

Help me see the treasure in the 'sand' of my life;
Heal me, free me, turn me around to see the wonder in the
    tired, weary, monotonous aspects of my life now;
Expand my limited way of looking, my restricted feeling of
    myself,
And do this for others, too, who I now name and ask that
    they know your blessing.   AMEN.

Prayer Activity

As if in one hand, 'hold' the aspects of your life that feel
like a wilderness in a negative way. In the other hand, 'hold'
abundant aspects of your life. Let each aspect speak their
truth: allow dialogue, both with each other and with Jesus.
Allow words of prayer to arise: of longing, of intention and
of hope.

Renewal

So we do not lose heart. Even though our outer nature is wasting away, our inner nature is being renewed day by day.

~ 2 Corinthians 4:16 ~

Prayer for Ourselves

Another day
for meeting new challenges,
for encountering new faces,
for undertaking the routine tasks
with renewed energy.
Another day
in which I am being remade
into the likeness of Jesus Christ,
hour by hour inwardly renewed.
Enable me, Lord,
to embrace the new day,
and to see it as a good friend
who will lead me nearer to you.

Prayer for Others

We pray today
for those who fear renewal:
those who live in the past,
those whose lives are a dead end,
those who are locked up in yesterday,
    who fear today,
    and cannot face tomorrow.
We pray too
for those who can no longer draw
    on their normal springs of renewal:
because they have lost their homes
    through natural disaster,
because they are separated from those they love
    through the cruelty of oppressors,
because they have lost hope
    through continual disappointment,
because they are in conflict
    with those who were once their friends.
Even when they feel they have lost much,
may they never lose heart.

Hannah

'Do not regard your servant as a worthless woman, for I have been speaking out of my great anxiety and vexation all this time.'

~ 1 Samuel 1:16 ~

Lord, be with me in my longing,
my yearning for you to remove the obstacles in my life,
to bring growth to my barren places within,
my desperateness to find my fulfilment,
to begin to realise my potential.

Lord, what is the missing link? What am I failing to do?
Is there something wrong with me?

Lord, bring me through the storm of my emotional turmoil.
Give me the courage to face and to watch
the swirl of my feelings, the confusion,
the distress that is in my mind and felt deep in my body.
Teach me, Lord, to be still in the midst of my questions.

Hear my cries – even if other people call me mad, or bad.
Hear my cries – for life, for birth, for release,
for possibility and new beginnings.

Lead me, help me find the people, the places, the
   connections
that will allow your life to flow in me and through me.
I dedicate this new birth to your Kingdom,
in this time, in this period of history –
that justice may come for me, for others.   AMEN.

Prayer Activity

'Healed are those who weep for their frustrated desire; they
shall see the face of fulfilment in a new form' (Matt 5:4,
translated from the Aramaic). Reflect on how this could be
for you today.

Jesus and Judas

'Why was this perfume not sold for three hundred denarii and the money given to the poor?'

~ John 12:5 ~

Sometimes I just can't keep up with you, Jesus.
One minute you talk about the poor,
the next you talk of banquets and feasting.
One minute you tell the rich young man to give up
    everything,
and the next you are producing more wine for the
    wedding.
One minute you said there will be poor with us always
and the next you are being bathed in expensive oil.

But then, maybe these moments call me to see beyond:
not seeking an immediate quick fix, but living into the
    future;
not solving a problem by throwing a solution at it, but
    choosing to live a more permanent way of justice.

Jesus, help me recognise the sacred moments
that call for a change in my living,
that call for a change in me.

May I now not imagine problem A will be solved with
  solution B,
or there is a formula to solve all the world's problems,
but that by living more justly,
I may be ready to celebrate goodness and hope when it
  happens,
knowing each is part of a lifetime's journey,
where I am called to give my whole life
to being an agent for change in the realm of love.

Prayer Activity

Being an agent of change begins with prayer. Tear out stories
of injustice from the paper today and paste them into a
scrap book or onto a sheet of paper and hold them with you
throughout the day and the rest of the week.

Blessing

Celebrate the wonder of God;
  celebrate the moments when heaven dances with earth;
  celebrate the doorways that set justice free;
  and live your life as that celebration, everyday.